"In the measured, understated lines of *Words for Coffee,* Tyler Robert Sheldon conjures the intimate, quiet, secure space of his grandmother's home. The speaker's beloved grandmother is cozy and known, but not simple: a radical therapist with a clear-headed bravery, she shares Rothkos and ancient oaks with the speaker, folding her strength into him. Later, as the poems delve into the heartache of memory loss and elder care, the speaker and his family 'pile sandbags against the coming flood,' imbued as they are with life from her gentle, empathetic presence. *Words for Coffee* channels the specific grief of a love that threatens perfection: the growing, collective awareness that it will someday end."

—Dorsey Craft, author of *A Brief History of Accidental Inventions* and *Plunder*

ALSO BY TYLER ROBERT SHELDON

Everything is Ghosts (Finishing Line Press, 2024)
When to Ask for Rain (Spartan Press, 2021)
Consolation Prize (Finishing Line Press, 2018)
Driving Together (Meadowlark Books, 2018)
Traumas (Yellow Flag Press, 2017)
First Breaths of Arrival (Oil Hill Press, 2016)

WITH JAMES BENGER

Against the Dark: Road Poems
(Stubborn Mule Press, 2019)

Words for Coffee

Poems by Tyler Robert Sheldon

Spartan
Press

Spartan Press
Kansas City, Missouri
Spartanpress.com

Spartan
Press

Copyright © Tyler Robert Sheldon, 2025
First Edition: 1 3 5 7 9 10 8 6 4 2
ISBN: 979-8-89975-020-5
LCCN: 2025945281

Author photo: Tyler Robert Sheldon

Acknowledgments:

Much love to my family, and to Alex, my muse.

With gratitude to Amy Sage Webb Baza, Azharuddin, Melanie Burdick, Liz Burk, Jimmy Butts, Anders Carlson-Wee, Chen Chen, Toby Daspit, Faith Ellington, Harley Elliott, Martha Garner, Dana Gioia, Kai Heck, Steven Hind, Amber Jurgensen, Walter Klumpp, Ted Kooser, Michelle Kreamer, Parker Logan, Denise Low, Clare and Dean Martin, Deb and Terry Maxwell, Patrice Melnick, Caryn Mirriam-Goldberg, Nonah Palmer, Kevin Rabas, Micah Romero, Chris Rovee, Jason Ryberg, Bessie and Tommy Senette, Vanessa Steinroetter, and Suzanne Wiltz.

Thanks to the editors of the following publications, who gave homes to the following poems, sometimes in earlier versions:

Comparative Woman – "A Recipe for Pumpkin Bread"
I-70 Review – "Photographs and Hurricane Francine"
Last Stanza Poetry Journal – "The Word for Coffee"
    "The Moon is Also Terrifyingly Real"
Slant – "Paper Cranes," "Rings, Mountain, Dress of Stars"

"In the Buffet Line at Anchor Inn, Autumn 2023" appeared in *The Poetry Harvest Project*, edited by Kansas Poet Laureate Traci Brimhall. Thanks to Traci for including my work.

"Reunion," "New Place," and "The TV's Out" appeared in the anthology *The Gasconade Review Presents: No One Sees the Irony,* from OAC Press. Thanks for Jason Ryberg for including those poems.

"Oregano Oil" appeared in a limited-edition cigar box art portfolio by Rich Wrobel. Great to work with you, man.

TABLE OF CONTENTS

III.

For Bev Sheldon.
I'll love you always.

Time offers this gift in its millions of ways.

-William Stafford

I.

MANTRA

I touched your toe, Grandma often tells me,
in the NICU after you were born. You were
here so early, the nurses told me not to, but
I'd already touched you, there was nothing
they could do, and even then I already knew
that everything would be just fine. It's true.

SINCE THE BEGINNING

Preschool, done in the bathroom,
I push open the door. There stand
two sneakered feet, familiar and waiting.
I look up, and up, and there she is,
in as a surprise from out of town,
waiting to take me to lunch—
my hero, the person whose sunny home
I know down to the inch,
whose very scent is comfort itself.
I run to my grandmother
and hug her as though she's
the absolute last person on earth.

CHOCOLATE PIE

at Thanksgiving, in Kansas City,
at my grandmother's yellow house. We
have a kid's table in the living room, just
the three of us, rulers of a little kingdom.
Nicky's big pie slice sits on its bright plate,
blue paper with snowmen, and he ladles on
whipped cream and grins. Logen's piece
is smaller as she runs a hand through
her dark and curly hair. And since I'm
the oldest, I wait until last.
                              The Christmas tree
is already up, the living room suspended
in yellow light, and in a few days it will snow.
Grandma laughs in the kitchen, hands me
a paper plate as I venture in for pie. Years
into the future, this is what I know: the tang
of dark chocolate stays in the nose, and on
the tongue and never leaves, like warm light
in a living room framed with the lowering
winter night outside. It brings me back
to my cousins' laughter, all of us too young
to know the world, our parents at the
grown-up table, and my grandmother
lifting dinner from the oven, making room
on the counter for one more thing
that brings us all together.

RINGS, MOUNTAIN, DRESS OF STARS

I flew with my family to attend a wedding. I was small.
More accurately now that I'm thinking about it I flew
with my family to be the ring-bearer in a wedding, for
my cousin, and before the big event—before the hike
up the side of a mountain, maybe actually just a large hill,
remember I was small, and it may have been an honest
to goodness mountain, but who's writing this, me or
you—and before the thinness of Colorado's air made us
all giddy, they outfitted me in a little tux, prepped me
on how to walk, to hold the pillow just so, balancing
the rings on its embroidered center like keeping them
there would ensure the marriage would last forever.
And then the trick would be doing all that halfway up
this mountain, so I sweated the whole thing a little bit,
and focused on my grandmother—not my cousin,
older than I and radiantly happy, just as one should be
at their wedding. Not my parents, tall and invincible, just
as parents should be when you're young enough
with big enough glasses to pass for Jonathan Lipnicki
in *Stuart Little*. I held the pillow and its rings and watched
only my grandmother, who smiled as the string lights
glinted off her earrings, whose long black dress glimmered
with still more tiny points of light, a night sky flowing
full with stars, and I walked—down to the end of that
rocky aisle, where the minister intoned his verse,
and where my cousin smiled down at me as
with both hands I lifted the pillow high.

A RECIPE FOR PUMPKIN BREAD

I.

Kansas City, middle autumn, at the pumpkin patch
and corn maze,

I wear a brand-new Chiefs puffer coat. I am maybe
six years old,

and the cold air needlepoints its way across my face,
stitching in

the morning. The grass is turning its way back into
earth, and every

single thing is gold. My cousins and I pick tiny oval
pumpkins

and wait for our turn at the giant wooden catapult,
the sun already

up and casting small shadows over the building with
its restrooms

and its gift shop, as my uncle helps Logen pull her
pumpkin back

in the big sling. They let it go, and the giant band
shoots forward,

and the little pumpkin flies and somewhere a field
over we think

we hear it land. Dad and I load my pumpkin next,
and everyone

steps back. Grandma watches as it climbs into the
new October air.

She laughs, and I imagine it fading all the way from
sight.

II.

The dry ingredients come first. My folks and I are
    in Grandma's kitchen

as she pulls the paper bag of flour from the
    cabinet overhead. This bread

rises through my childhood, so when I think
    pumpkin I think *Kansas*

City, I think *Grandma's house*, with its sunny yellow
    walls, and so some

part of my deepest self is perpetually fall. Mom
    asks about the office,

the clients who seek her out for therapy, as
    Grandma sifts the flour

into a giant yellow bowl. But I am young, and
    Grandma knows, and says

only so much. There are still more ingredients to
    go. Only later

will I hear about the man who pulled the gun.

III.

Sugar never touches Grandma's coffee, and only
    at her house do I ever

drink it black. Alex and I are not yet married, still
    in college, up

from campus for the weekend, and we sit on the
    orange floral couch

while from the kitchen we hear the coffee maker
    percolate its patient way.

We talk about what we'll do once up and
    moving—Grandma wants to

take us to the art museum, with its giant
    shuttlecocks upon the vast
green lawn. She gets up to pour the coffee.
    I follow her into the kitchen,
measure out two spoons of sugar, to bring
    balance to this drink
that I've always imagined as strong enough to
    wake the dead.

The museum is full of Rothkos, their giant fields
    of color designed to calm
at the atomic level, and this is what I'm looking
    forward to the most.
Alex likes Rothko too, but can't stand Benton,
    and so of course what greets
us first is the man with a gun, over his shoulder
    and long as time feels
on a sugar high. Beside him in this painting strides
    a behatted boy,
powder horn slung across his shoulders, his gaze
    forward
toward a moment none of us can see.

IV.
Cloves are like little hands without a body. They
    fumble their way
into your own palm, in third grade, as with your
    other hand you lift
an orange in its textured skin. You dot these little

hands all over,
and suddenly the orange smells like fall, though
    outside in the cold
the first flakes swirl down toward the classroom.
    To finish
you tie a piece of yarn to this new ornament's stem,
    prepare to
make another, perfect gifts for family, and Grandma
    will hang hers
on the tree in Kansas City, and this too will rise
    throughout your
memories like bread baking in a kitchen.

V.
Cinnamon tea waits
in the kitchen cabinet
as we all choose its neighbors
first, then close the door
and leave it in the dark.
Grandma's teapot whistles
and still it waits, like
a memory, fading over time.

VI.
Eggs, crack-crack, into the big bowl.
Grandma stirs, pours in the milk,
and we pull the loaf pan from the cabinet,
the oven hot and waiting. Before long
we'll all sit down and slice up this bread,
so aromatic you'd think a pumpkin patch
was waiting right around the corner.

VII.
Butter
in little glass dishes, perfect
round pats, to sit atop the bread.
Butter-yellow ceramic swans
above the china cabinet.
They look down and
witness as we laugh
and cut another slice.

KANSAS CITY'S BIGGEST TREE

Outside my grandmother's house
stands the most colossal tree in Kansas City,

planted the year she was born. She tells us
that this huge oak, with acorns whose lids

were big enough for my childhood G.I. Joe
to use as hats, made her screech to a halt

before the For Sale sign out front and
insist to the realtor that she simply *had*

to own the house. *I can't leave*
that tree alone now that I've met it,

she told him, with its branches
stretching farther than the house's roof

itself could span. We all played as kids
around its giant roots. And to this day it lives.

RED BIRDS

When the big hand is on the twelve
which is also a cardinal, Grandma's
favorite bird, if you stand just outside
the yellow kitchen doorway you'll hear
the red birds singing. Grandma waits

at the window in the kitchen
as this clock ticks on between
the hours, and cardinals flit
their scarlet way up to the sill.

They sit and watch her with their tiny
black eyes. They are so vivid and so
real that everything outside
of their little crimson beings
could be just one birdly dream.

THE MOON IS ALSO TERRIFYINGLY REAL

Grandma puts on a VHS tape
in the back room. I am a child
of maybe five. On the tape, a boy
finds a rabbit in the attic. A thrill.
But this is before the boy falls ill.

The doctor takes
the velveteen rabbit
away to be burned.
A veritable mass
of germs, that will sit
in the rubbish bin
under the full, pale moon,
that above all must go.

But the little toy soldiers
hatch a plan to save the rabbit
and the Skin Horse
encourages the whole thing,
wishing more than
anything for the rabbit
to be just as real
as it wants. The horse also
warns the fear-eyed rabbit
that realness is forever.

As a child I cheered
when the fairy changed

the rabbit in the end. He was
hopping real, twitching-whisker
real, a super-rabbit. I wanted
nothing more than to be so real.

But the world around
the rabbit was also real,
too real, and the moon
goes away each night
and briefly it is fully dark,
and maybe we are not
quite rabbit enough.

THE HARE AND THE HEDGEHOG

Grandma puts on another VHS tape
in the back room. I am a child still.
On the tape, a man, and rolling hills.

The old man sits
just outside the village
with the children all around.

His red hat covers his eyes
and a smile twitches
in his wizardly white beard

as they tell him that they've heard
this one before, and has he run
out of stories? The old man

says of course not, you little shits—
no no, he says just wait, hold on
to your butts, cigarette twitching

in his mouth, but my bad, that's Sam
Jackson in *Jurassic Park*—okay,
he says, let me tell you all about

this little family of hedgehogs.
They live near a turnip patch in a field
owned by a farmer, and ohmygod,

those turnips will haunt you for your
entire childhood, nothing else could
possibly taste so good as when the father

hedgie hooks his teeth into the soft
white flesh of a turnip the proportionate
size of a backyard shed. In much more

proper language the old man tells
the children too about the rabbit
who lives in the next-door field, who

lords it over a cabbage patch—not as good
as turnips, say the hedgehogs, but not
bad—and who dares the father hedgehog

to a race. So what Mr. Hog does, he gets
his wife and son, and they post up at the end
of the cabbage rows, and because all

hedgies look alike to Mr. Rabbit—because
he's not that politically correct, so be better,
dear children—the rabbit, quick

as a heart attack down the rows again and again,
finds one of the family every stop. It might
as well have been the Hedgehog Godfather,

because look at how they massacred
our boy, and in the fullness of time
the rabbit falls into his own green crop,

mind fixed only on one hedgehog, knowing
fully nothing of the family, ears deflated
like cabbage leaves in summer heat.

And so, dear children, says the old man,
a clever mind is faster, no matter what
they say, than even the quickest feet.

Grandma comes back in from the front room,
mouths the man's last words. The credits roll.
She too has a mind that can't be beat.

WICKER

The furniture in Grandma's guest room
is all white, painted wicker. As a child
I set my small suitcase at the foot
of a wicker bed, my book on a sturdy
wicker dresser, and my glasses, before sleep,
on a wicker table standing just inside

the door. I could hear the bird clock
ticking in the kitchen through the night,
one of my favorite sounds—it meant
everything was right, my red hair
brushing the stiff and braided headboard,
my father as a child in a frame up on the wall,

the next day's possibilities flashing through my mind,
the pale moon in the window, filtering through the blinds.

RADICAL

Your father reads in multiple languages. Compared
to what the average American is used to, this is
absolutely a superpower, so we all have a high bar

to jump for. He also ministers at the First English
Lutheran Church and will spread the good word
from the War until the eighties, a neat forty years.

Chain yourself to the university president's door
until he agrees to meet with you about your ideas.
Do this in the hippie years, so it's even cooler

later. Manage apartments while getting
your master's, because doesn't everyone?
Visit your clients at their homes, even

the ones with dirt floors and no lights, and
leave before the start of fights, but only
if you're truly sure you can't stop them.

That still life hanging above the dining room table,
its basket of fruit, the eggplant and tomato vying
for control? The library's. I didn't know for years.

Turn around while halfway back to Kansas City
after Christmas, knock on the door, and say you're
here for New Year's too. We'd have it no other way.

ICE CREAM THERAPY

The truth is, Grandma tells me on the phone, most every
thing can be fixed with a Frosty. If you can't get Wendy's,
just get ice cream, your favorite kind. It's what I tell all
my clients—wouldn't you feel a bit better with a small
treat, just to settle back into yourself for the afternoon,
some cold and creamy happiness on the end of a spoon?

One time a client cussed me out, he even pulled a gun.
I told him, there's the door, don't talk to anyone
until you've gotten a Frosty and taken the time
to linger on each spoonful. If you feel better, fine—
make another appointment, and we'll talk more then.
She tells me they usually come back with a grin,

ready to tell her where it hurts, why they feel this way.
This work is hard, she says. You must make room for play.

WORDS FOR COFFEE

This is our morning trade: words
for coffee, passing each across
the table. Our plans for the day
billow forth like smiles, like
sun rays, like fragrant, waiting steam.

ANGEL FOOD CAKE

I.
This is what families take to their graves. The recipe
for a cake so light you could lift yourself on its fluffy
white wings all the way to the moon. This is not really
a cake. This is sensory input encoded into the deepest
parts of the self, what you gather when the sun won't
come out, this is a dopamine hit in a pan. This is
a building block of life, and so you should be careful.
Life is like that. Be brave, but beware. If you whisk
the egg whites too much, everything will collapse.

II.
Grandma takes the pan out of the oven. Inside, the cake
sleeps, a small white creature in a dense brown jacket,
hiding from the world outside, which will rip it
apart because the world too needs sustenance and this
is how the food chain works, baby, don't let anyone
catch you sleeping, but the cake hears nothing of our
anticipatory breathing, doesn't see the knife, shiny like
a fox's claw, the pan beneath clear like ice, like a frozen
pond, so extreme in sensation that hot and cold become
one.

III.
We've all savored
this cake for years.
One evening one of us
finds the box in the trash,

its recipe on the back
like an incantation,
one written by others,
but still the spell holds.

IV.
The best cakes always have secrets. They become
memories, lock themselves in, and memories
kept from the self are the innermost sanctum of
secret, like someone has opened us up, and taken
us out, and has placed us on the counter while
turning to the fridge, setting the box down
for later, where it becomes just a part
of the kitchen, invisible in plain sight.

OREGANO OIL

This is not, despite what
Grandma suggests, the elixir
of life. You will not wake up
cured of your loneliness, your
deepest ills. But you may

find connection to some deeper
part of the world older than your
self. You will heal quickly from colds.
You will also smell like pizza
while doing so.

Good for almost, it seems, every
other thing, like ice cream for unruly
other people, and for happy days alike.
Despite what later comes, these methods stay:
when spiders or fire walk into your life,

Grandma says, hold this up against them
to watch their inflictions melt away.
So you take the bottle with its dropper
from the shelf, and place one drop
at a time beneath your tongue, and on

your wounds, and wait, and will
yourself back to the days when

she brought you the little bottle
in one warm hand and healed
you with a smile.

THE IDEAL TIMELINE

Grandma takes us to the museum. She gets tickets,
calls us to the counter, and the woman on the other side
is from Louisiana, the same town where my wife and I
now live, and what a small world it is. Grandma smiles,
tells her how glad she is that we are here, up from
the South and back in the arms of family. And so
we get our tickets for half price, small-world perks.

In the next room: Lichtenstein and Johns, explosions
and flags and color and the slow unsticking of time
as I hold my wife's hand, my other arm around
Grandma's shoulders, and as I imagine the future:
all of us at her house in Kansas City, morning
coffee steaming, light climbing across the floor
in pointillist pop-art dots, like static, like snow.
We are happy. We all remember, and we all know.

II.

PAPER CRANES

I.

I pull one square red page
out of the sleeve. Years before,
at ten, I pull another, just like
this one, free from the plastic
and fold, and pull and fold,
until a dozen little birds await
on my grandmother's
dining room table. The fan
in her office spins the birds
for years in one big circle,
tethered to their mobile,
which is tethered to
the ceiling that overlooks
her life helping others heal.
Clients haul their pain
into her office, cradle it
like paper, and above them
while they talk, the cranes
spin like the needle
of a compass that wants
everything at once.
They continue watching
in their patterned smallness
when she packs the office,
moves books and papers home,
and they continue watching

as we pull into town,
pull our bags out of the car,
and pull her close to hug her.

II.
I fold the red paper
along one corner, building
a hypotenuse, a path of
least distance which
when I'm finished
is suddenly sharp
at either end. I fold the page
the other way, and the X
marks the new place
my grandmother will live,
close enough for family
on happy days, or
for emergencies. She will make
new friends on her floor,
be the youngest one there,
and will get up to, so I hear,
all the best kinds of trouble.

III.
Three more folds
and wings unfurl
from this thing
that was once paper
and is almost but
not quite yet a bird.

IV.

She gets new glasses.
All the better to see
us with; unfolds the arms
to set upon her ears,
the world a little
sharper, like paper
turning in the sun.

V.

The last fold conjures
as if from nothing
the delicate beak, the
most crucial step,
where one must crease
the paper into its
wondrously tiny point
with a fingernail,
then wait. After all
this time, now at last
the crane can breathe.

VI.

Paper cranes are gentle,
their sharp points an illusion.
Just like us, they will wait forever
for the perfect hand to hold them.
They all want light to find them
through the dust motes
of an early autumn afternoon.
Paper cranes are gentle.
They are more like glass than steel.

RITUAL, LIKE AN APOTROPAIC CHARM

Before the move, Grandma begins
forgetting: names, friends, family,
but recalls smells, coffee dark
& reassuring in her yellow cup,
a tether when the sun comes up.

HOME OFFICE

The writing desk waits. Atop it
sits what Grandma would transform
into her chronicle of self—she writes
such essays every decade—but now
is the simplest arrangement of items:
the yellow coffee cup, full not with drink
but with ink pens, this one from the bank,
this one a gift from my father, nib shrouded
in a lid which caps its liquid potential,
but only for now, only until everything
is ready. And here, the chair I swiveled in
as a kid, the chair which goes too far back,
its wooden seat and springs alight
with the danger of it, the way gravity, like
time, faithfully does its quiet part and waits.
On the wall above the desk, a plaque of wood,
its quote a line from Cinderella: *One shoe
can change your life.* But the shoe, to mean
anything, must be forgotten, must stir
the mind like gravity stirs a body
in a wooden chair, like a spoon stirs
coffee in its cup. And all of this must fit,
must mean it, must open like a book,
a journal, like this one here, also resting
atop Grandma's desk, to welcome
any shining thing that still waits to come.

THE WORD FOR COFFEE

The barista, just a bit younger than me,
makes his home above a church, tells me
this way he can walk to work. He
steps out from around the counter
in brand new thick-soled Chelseas.

He has to grind some beans, make this shop
smell like cozy winter burning, the kind
you scent when on a walk in a Midwest
December redolent with the threat of snow.
Done, he brings a bag of these to the counter,

dips a hand in, lifts out some of what he's made.
He asks me to lean in and whiff them,
carrying the memory of their country across
the ocean to my nose, and for a moment I
forget the world outside this shop, and even

that states away, in a Midwest winter,
my grandmother takes longer to recall the word
for coffee, the name of a church downstreet,
clinging to the scents of the world as their names
get up and step away and grind themselves to dust.

STAIRS

Grandma makes her careful way
to the basement once a week
or more. When visiting I do this
for her. Whoever goes down

to this pillared, cave-cold room
hauls along the basket, brimming
with its clothes, to where the washer
waits in the cold and concrete dark.

One then starts the load, and lifts
the basket, ghostly in the single
swinging light. The clothes and you

who've brought them here are pale.
You start back for the stairs,
oh so tall and with no rail.

ELECTION SEASON

"That man on TV," Grandma says.
We sit in her back room. "Why does he
have to be so mean?" For months
she has railed against this politician,

cursed his inhumane ideas, his name,
her heart pounding for the people
he would hurt, and now that name
is a headline in a newspaper

full with bad tidings and blown
down the street like a leaf
among so many leaves
in the breath of the coming storm.

Amid it all, we do not know
what we can say, sitting with her
on the back room couch.
On TV, the crowd applauds.

I get up to make coffee.
Grandma follows, anything
to get away.

STRAY, VERB

I hear the meow and hang up the phone. This
    tabby
that's been coming around has the same name
    from

two of my neighbors. To Beth this gray kitty is
    Andrew.
Hannah around back names him Andy. They arrive

at these names quietly, without any discussion, like
    how
strays find their ways into your home and adopt
    you.

Or how eight hundred miles away, the forgetting
slinks catlike into my grandmother's mind. I
    imagine

that as she also hangs up the phone, she leans back
and smiles, and closes her eyes in the blinds-filtered
    sun.

MOVING DAY

Everything fits into this little yellow house.
The birds in their mobile, the birds
in their clock, the cardinals at the window,
the cardinal at twelve. When the big hand
brushes the bright plumage, painted in,
and the red bird sings, everything
we know will change.

REUNION

Grandma at last sells her home. She's older
and forgetting. She moves to my hometown,
unpacks the couch, and later introduces
herself to my sister, very glad to
meet her, make new friends.

VISIT

October 2023

I get on a plane to see her. Before takeoff,
on the phone, she just can't wait—she'll
introduce me to all her new friends,
has lots of news. When I hang up the phone,
the sun slants over the wing like a smile,
and through the window, and breaks
into a rainbow through my tears.

AIRPORT TIME

My parents pick me up. We walk
through the terminals, through
the lobby, to the car, and she's not far
from our minds, her smile balanced
now with how things change
almost daily, so I've heard, like foils

on the wings of planes, small movements
within a space that never changes
until suddenly everything does,
like airport time, how you step
outside into what you expect
is the glorious sunset only to find

a difference that couldn't be more stark:
that in a blink the air is fully dark.

IN THE BUFFET LINE AT ANCHOR INN, AUTUMN 2023

I stack the enchiladas on my orange plate carefully,
like / I'm building a house, and the line / moves
a bit here in the Anchor Inn, the restaurant of
my childhood / in the town where I've returned, /
where I am back to see my grandmother, who stands /
next to me, who is / fading, so I've heard, so far
north / of Louisiana, where I've made my new home.
/ What kills me isn't how / she doesn't remember,
because she does—she / recalls my childhood, every
visit we've had together, / the mornings with coffee in
the living room, / so strong because she perhaps alone
among all people / thought it proper to double the
ratio of coffee grounds / to water. Now when I want
to wake up and really mean it / I make Grandma
Coffee, just like this. And / she still knows the cheesy
tang of these / enchiladas, the smoky fried potato tacos
/ just a little further down this line. No, / what makes
me tear up as if from too much / of this restaurant's
hot sauce is how she / spins it all, uses synonyms for
words she can't recall, / almost sells it. My sister
becomes "your friend" when we talk, / and when I visit
her assisted living apartment / the next day, she will
insist / on making the coffee, that she doesn't need to
/ and will not stop, her body, / her mind a house that
will never / ever be blown down. Ahead of me / in line,
she tong-lifts a small potato taco, / holds it before her like
a wonder of the world / that she's never seen before.

NEW PLACE

At the assisted living complex, so cheery
it could be a hip new hotel, my grandmother waits
by the front door for Mom and Dad and me to arrive.
I've been up since seven, she tells us, smiling
and bouncing a little from excitement. *I just
couldn't wait to see you. What would you like
to do?* We say *we'd love to hang out at your place,
Grandma,* and it's true—this apartment rings
with the familiar tone of her former home,
its '70s floral couch and china cabinet, the huge
round coffee table fit for all of Arthur's knights.

She has NPR on the radio when we all get there,
this cozy room with its happy yellow paint,
so like the old place, and Grandma turns up
the dimmer switch. Mom and Dad sit in rockers
that I've known since I was born, and before
we take the couch, Grandma gives my shoulder
a squeeze. The sun climbs its way through
the wall-length window's blinds. Though it's
not the place we knew, it feels just as safe as home.

THE TV'S OUT

October 2023

and so Grandma and I sit
on the bomb-proof floral couch,
which we say will surely be here
after all that's left is the horizon
and the venerable cockroach,
and we listen to the radio. Across
the world, terrorists attack Israel.
The folks on NPR stay calm.
Nothing they can say will change
the state of things. I get up
to grab some ice cream from
the fridge, make up two bowls,
and bring it over. Grandma smiles,
spoons up a small bite. She says,
the cable guy won't be here until
next week. On the radio, gunfire.
In the black mirror of the sleeping
TV set, the two of us, arms across
each other's shoulders, listening.

SUNGLASSES

I.

To get downstairs and out the door
to the big wood rockers waiting for us
in the sun, first we stand up from the couch
like two sails in a breeze. We make our way
to the table by the door, grab keys, head out
into the hallway, and take steps in sync like
it's a game, all the way to the elevator.

We wave hello to Toni at the front desk. The doors
rush open—I wave my fingers like Obi-Wan
Kenobi, I use the Force, and Grandma laughs.
We pace slowly over to the big wood chairs,
and sit, and one of us has forgotten their shades
in the room upstairs, and for once it isn't me.
Too bright to stay, we make our way inside.

II.

Grandma goes right to them, but I,
who can't find my hapless way out
of a wet paper bag without a map,
look in the closet, on the kitchen table,
on the bureau, beside the coffee pot.
Grandma holds her blue sunglasses
in one hand, and smiles, entertained
and in no rush.

III.

We sit, at last, in the rockers.
The sun is perfect, a tiny coin
through our lenses, just shiny
enough to stop you on the street
to pick it up and make a wish.

MANTRA

Back in Baton Rouge, the next day off the plane, I call
her on the phone, and her *Hel-lo?* across the miles is
its Audrey Hepburn tone, just as it's been for years,
and I tell her that I'm home. She's been up again
since seven, already wishes I were here. She's making
coffee, doesn't say how many scoops. *Your father's
coming to see me,* she says, and I can hear her spoon
stir in the sugar. *I love that man. And I love you, Tyler.
I've loved you since that first day,
when I touched your toe.*
                              Wish I could be there,
I tell her, and I can almost hear it as she smiles. *Call me
any time,* she says. I go into the kitchen, fill the coffee pot,
measure out how many scoops, and we stay there
on the phone. We drink our coffee. A red bird flashes
past the window. Everything, for now, will be
just fine. It's true.

III.

PHOTOGRAPHS AND HURRICANE
FRANCINE

The day my father calls with the news,
a hurricane barrels into Baton Rouge.
The family sends each other photos:
in this one, Grandma wears John Lennon shades,
her curled hair silver, the sun at her back.
We pile sandbags against the coming flood.

In this one, she holds baby me, knows
some secret, smiles in her gentle way.
In this one she shares a midday snack.
Crepe myrtles offer up their deep pink buds.
I walk the rainy road between their rows.

Before the storm the sunlight fades,
rain lances down, and I turn back.
In this one, she holds out her arms for a hug.

We tell each other to take this slow.
We all remember, and we all know.

BLACKBERRY TEA

My cats have found the end of their dispute.
The little void, so very black his eyes
float amid the midnight of his face, keeps

a wary green orb fixed on the spunky
older tortoiseshell. She swats and nips
his tail, despite just reaching middle age.

The sort of scene my grandmother, gone now
these six months, would have chuckled
about in her Audrey Hepburn tone,

bringing coffee in from the kitchen
steaming in its happy yellow cups. But
at last it's time for something different,

and the cats, all grumbles, let me up.
The kettle whistles, lets out its shrill hoot.
My cup is ready, its teabag redolent of fruit.

Tyler Robert Sheldon is the author of seven other poetry collections including *Everything is Ghosts* (Finishing Line Press, 2024) and *When to Ask for Rain* (Spartan Press, 2021), a Birdy Poetry Prize Finalist. He is Editor-in-Chief of *MockingHeart Review* and an editor at *Dialogue: The Interdisciplinary Journal of Pop Culture and Pedagogy*, and his work has appeared in *Dialogue, The Midwest Quarterly, The Los Angeles Review, Ninth Letter, Pleiades, Slant, Tinderbox Poetry Journal,* and other places. His research interests include poetry and poetics, comics studies, pedagogy, and World War II. A Pushcart Prize nominee and winner of the

Charles E. Walton Essay Award as well as several awards for his teaching. Sheldon earned his PhD at LSU and his MFA at McNeese State University. He spends his days teaching, writing, playing guitar, and catering to the whims of his impish cats. View his work at TylerRobertSheldon com.

This project was made possible, in part, by generous support from the Osage Arts Community.

Osage Arts Community provides temporary time, space and support for the creation of new artistic works in a retreat format, serving creative people of all kinds — visual artists, composers, poets, fiction and nonfiction writers. Located on a 152-acre farm in an isolated rural mountainside setting in Central Missouri and bordered by ¾ of a mile of the Gasconade River, OAC provides residencies to those working alone, as well as welcoming collaborative teams, offering living space and workspace in a country environment to emerging and mid-career artists. For more information, visit us at www.osageac.org

Osage Arts Community